BABA THAKUR SINGH BHINDRANWALE

ISHWAR SINGH

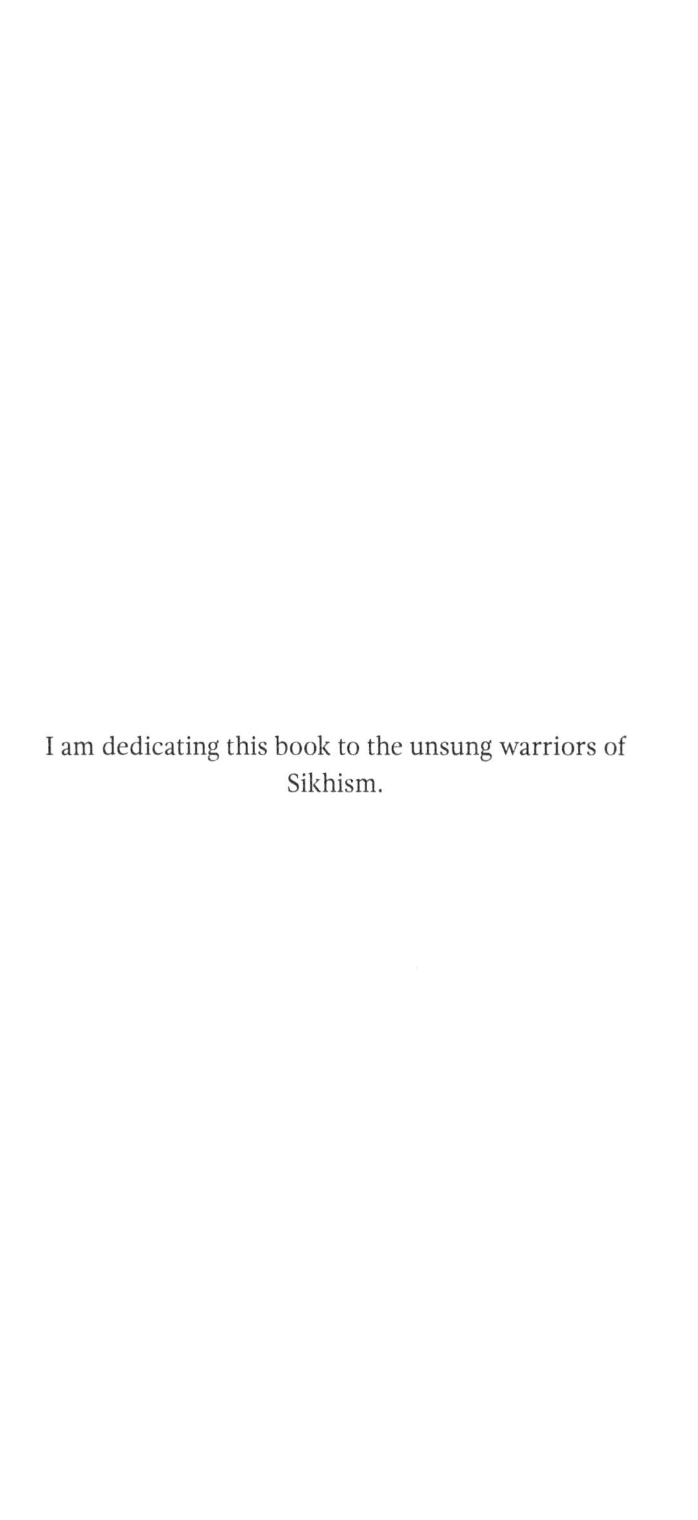

I am dedicating this book to the unsung warriors of Sikhism.

Contents

Foreword

Ishwar Singh have more than ten years of experience in writing story books, sakhis of devotional saints and in research activities. He is a tremendous writer. He is doing excellent job by writing about the brief biography of Baba Thakur Singh Bhindranwale. He had shown very keen interest in the field of religious resources and other cultural issues.

He is also a very excellent teacher and also having deep knowledge about the social science issues. I have always seen him working very hard for his various books. He just want to express about the Indian culture to our new generations in a simple and brief manner. I wish him all the very best for his new book.

Birinder Pal Kaur

Preface

This book is about the brief biography of Baba Thakur Singh Bhindranwale. The task behind to publish such content is to spread knowledge about the unsung heroes of the Sikh history among the new generation. In the schools, which are being organised by Sikh trusts, the students are just getting very limited knowledge about the Sikh warriors. Baba Banda Singh Bahadur, Baba Deep Singh etc. are the common names on the tongues of the students but they don't know about the others. This is just an effort to spread this brief information among new generations. I hope that you will like this book.

Acknowledgements

Writing a book is harder than I thought and more rewarding than I could have ever imagined. None of this would have been possible without my best friend, my teacher, my best motivator, my beloved mother Amarjit Kaur. She was the first who inspired me for my goals and taught me various subjects and created my interest specially in Social Sciences. She stood by me during every struggle and all my successes. Whatever I had achieved in my life it is due to my mother.

I'm eternally grateful to my father Pal Singh, who took in an extra mouth to feed when he didn't have to. He taught me discipline, tough love, manners, respect, and so much more that has helped me succeed in life. I truly have no idea where I'd be if he hadn't given me a roof over my head whom I desperately needed at that age.

To my father-in-law Narinder Singh for their moral support during the up and downs in my life. He taught me how to live positive even in the worst situations by sharing his personal experiances. He is the man who suggest me to write a book in your life because it will be your book by which you will be remembered in future.

To Dr. Davinder Singh, who never saw my age, my race, or my lack of formal education. He just saw a kid hungry to learn, hungry to grow, and hungry to succeed in teaching. He never stopped me; he only encouraged me.

Prologue

In present day life, every one is playing his role according to the role assingned by the nature. I have very much interest to explore various great warriors or personalities and cultural aspects of our Indian Society. So an idea came in my mind to explore the brief biography of Baba Thakur Singh Bhindranwale. I am writing this book for our younger generations so that when they will read this book, they must understand the sacrifices of our forefathers.

CHAPTER ONE

BABA THAKUR SINGH BHINDRANWALE

Baba Thakur Singh Ji was born in 1915 to revered parents Baba Bahadur Singh and Mata Prem Kaur Ji in the Pakistani town of Eechogill, District Lahore. His parents were also Amritdharis who performed several daily prayers and had unwavering faith in the guru.

They arrived in India after the partition and set up residence in the village of Sadaruala near Makhu District Ferozepur. Baba Ji had unwavering confidence in the Guru and meditated continuously his entire life. He was also kind, serene, and infused with spiritual energy. They would not squander their time talking or playing while they were young.

They began assisting his parents when they were a little older, and as a result, he was permanently tuned in to the one intoxicating Naam Simran. Baba Ji has always been inspired to help others when immersed in seva and simran. He used to give his money, food, and possessions with others since he was a little child because he saw the light of God in everything. Baba Ji's desire to experience the presence and service of a genuine Gursikh as overwhelming.

The Brahmgiani Sant Gurbachan Singh Ji Khalsa and his Jatha, who are regarded as brilliant intellectuals and who have the blessings of Satguru Sri Guru Gobind Singh Ji, were practising Sikhi Parchar, they discovered through others. Khalsa Ji lived at Bhindran in District Moga, therefore Baba Ji left his house and went there. Amrit was taken from Panj Pyare there by Baba Ji. Khalsa Ji appointed Baba Ji as Langar's manager after recognising his spiritual condition. This seva was carried out with great devotion and love. After serving for two and a half years, Khalsa Ji welcomed Baba Ji into the Jatha and instructed him in the ways of God.

Before Khalsa Ji moved to Sachkand, Baba Ji spent 22 years performing seva for Garveye (a close colleague). Khalsa Ji, pleased with this seva, showered Baba Ji with numerous presents. They bestowed to him a wonderful spiritual condition. They predicted that you will one day carry out the greatest act of service ever. Following Khalsa Ji's departure for Sachkand, Baba Jee continued to perform Langer and sangat services alongside Sant Giani Kartar Singh Jee Khalsa and perpetually retained his Naam Simran imprint. Sant Giani Kartar Singh Ji had a great deal of respect for Baba Ji and frequently talked with him about important decisions.

For Sikhs, this was a crucial time since numerous attempts were being made to suppress the Sikh community as a political and religious movement. Sant Kartar Singh Ji Khalsa organised 37 significant processions that alerted the dozing Sikh population to who they were. Sant Kartar Singh

Ji Khalsa was being targeted by the authorities in an effort to silence him. In response, Sant Ji said the following:

"In the event of my arrest by the authorities, Baba Takhur Singh Ji would then be in charge of Damdami Taksal. Whoever they choose can receive the seva of leadership."

Sant Giani Jarnail Singh Ji Khalsa was chosen by Baba Ji to lead the Damdami Taksal after Sant Kartar Singh Ji Khalsa Bhindranwale was elevated to Sachkand. Sant Ji would follow Baba Ji's guidance without fail. To rescue the Sikhs from government tyranny, Sant Jarnail Singh Ji Khalsa launched the Dharam Yudh Morcha in July 1982. He established Amritsar as his permanent home, and Baba Ji was granted the seva to care for Gurudwara Gurdarshan Parkash, Mehta. Numerous Singhs and Singhnia were martyred in June 1984 when the government assaulted Sri Harmander Sahib and Sri Akal Takht Sahib. The Damdami Taksal was given to Baba Ji by the Sangat to carry out in Sant Ji's absence after the attack, and they are now doing so to the best of their abilities. Baba Ji has led the Damdami Taksal through trying and challenging times, and his wisdom has shone through throughout.

Baba Ji regularly visits events all over the world and has maintained the Damdami Taksal Parchar. Numerous people have received Amrit and been inspired by Baba Ji's parchar. He has defended the legal rights of Singhs who have been detained and helped those who are still incarcerated in any way he could. Shaheed's families have been supported and are currently being supported.

He revived the revered Sarbat Khalsa tradition, and they rebuilt Sri Akal Takht Sahib with great physical zeal. Since then, several more Gurudwaras have been constructed or are undergoing renovation.

In Sri Amritsar, Gurdwara Shaheed Ganj B-block was constructed in honour of the Shaheeds who lost their lives in the 1978 encounter with the Nakali Nirankaris. A Gurdwara was constructed at Sri Anandpur Sahib on Kiratpur Sahib Road for the benefit of travelling sangats. An academy and hospital dedicated to the Khalsa have been constructed in Mehta in honour of Sant Giani Gurbachan Singh Ji Khalsa. In the panth, Baba Ji is revered as a profoundly spiritual and gifted leader who is also a shining example of a Khalsa.

After a brief illness, Baba Thakur Singh passed away on December 24th, 2004 at a nearby private hospital. His age was 89.

Baba Thakur Singh Bhindranwale

Baba Ji at Harimandar Sahib

Conclusion

Under the mild direction of Baba Thakur Singh, Damdami Taksal, which was known as the "nursery of militancy" during the rule of Sant Bhindranwale, experienced good days. Despite being a quiet man, he stirred up trouble by saying that Sant Bhindranwale had fled during the Army raid in June 1984 and was "in excellent spirits."

Although Baba Thakur Singh, a fervent proponent of this philosophy, is no longer with us, Damdami Taksal was split over this issue. Sant Bhindranwale, according to Baba Ji, would return one day and succeed as the Jathedar of Damdami Taksal.

Those who contend that Sant Bhindranwale was executed during Operation Bluestar, however, are of the opinion that after the Baba's passing, no one will fall into their theory.

At Akal Takht, eight extremist organisations claiming to be Shaheed Jarnail Singh and the Ghallughara Yaadgar Committee had already hailed Sant Bhindranwale as a "martyr." When Sant Bhindranwale was recognised as a "martyr," the Jathedar, Akal Takht, Giani Joginder Singh Vedanti, and senior members of the S.G.P.C. were there. Bhai Isher Singh, the older son of Sant Bhindranwale, had accepted a siropa from Jathedar Vedanti, making it abundantly evident that his family had come to terms with the Sant's death during Operation Bluestar.